SEX: A Christian Perspective

A 4-week course to help senior highers make responsible sex decisions

by Walt Marcum

Group®
Loveland, Colorado

Sex: A Christian Perspective
Copyright © 1990 by Group Publishing, Inc.

Fourth Printing, 1992

Credits
Edited by Stephen Parolini
Cover designed by Jill Bendykowski and DeWain Stoll
Interior designed by Judy Atwood Bienick and Jan Aufdemberge
Cover photo by David Priest
Illustrations by Judy Atwood Bienick
Photo on p. 9 by David Priest
Photos on pp. 18 and 34 by Brenda Rundback

ISBN 1-55945-206-4
Printed in the United States of America

CONTENTS

INTRODUCTION 4
Sex: A Christian Perspective

COURSE OBJECTIVES....................5

HOW TO USE THIS COURSE............6

THIS COURSE AT A GLANCE............8

PUBLICITY PAGE 9

LESSON 1 11
Sex and Sexuality
Help senior highers understand and appreciate the difference between sex and sexuality.

LESSON 2 20
The Virtues of Waiting
Help senior highers understand why the Christian faith says to save sex for marriage.

LESSON 3 28
How to Say No to Sexual Pressure
Help senior highers learn how to resist sexual pressure.

LESSON 4 35
Dangers of Playing Around
Help senior highers understand the dangers and consequences associated with sex.

BONUS IDEAS 43

SEX: A CHRISTIAN PERSPECTIVE

Teenage girl: It happens. You go to a party and you have sex with a guy and that's that. And you do it at [age] 14 or 15.

Reporter: And more likely than not, you're doing it with or without contraception?

All teenagers: Without. Definitely without.

Reporter: Are there a lot of abortions?

Teenage girl: Yes, it's the main way to escape.

Teenage boy: Almost a form of birth control.

Reporter: Is there such a thing as a relationship without sex?

[Silence.]

Reporter: Is AIDS something people your age think about?

All teenagers: Yes. Definitely. But you think it could never happen to you.

Does this conversation shock you? surprise you? This conversation, which aired on a national TV-news program, is both an indictment against and a challenge to our sex education methods.

The young people in your Sunday school class already receive sex education. They get it from movies, magazines, song lyrics and television. They learn about sexuality and sexual values in jokes, on bathroom walls, in the back seats of cars and in the back bedrooms at parties.

There's plenty of sex education going on in our culture. But is the Christian perspective a part of that education? Are teenagers exposed to a healthy, biblical view of sex and sexuality?

The evidence indicates that today's youth listen to the culture and its values—and not the church and its values. A TV report on contemporary sexual behavior of adolescents announced that half of America's teenagers are sexually active—resulting in a million pregnancies a year. The number of teenagers with the AIDS virus and other venereal diseases is climbing.

Behind these statistics lie untold pain and suffering. Teenagers are making sexual decisions. And many of their decisions have long-lasting consequences.

Some people in the church believe our kids are somehow different. We look at the young people sitting in our Sunday school class and think they know better. But a recent survey of conservative Christian teenagers gives some insight about when our kids may become sexually active.

Percent of church youth who admit to having sexual intercourse.

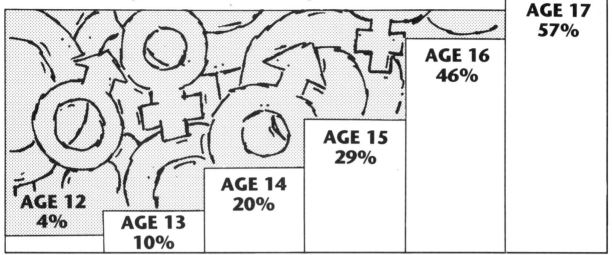

According to this survey, between one-third and two-thirds of the teenagers sitting in our senior high Sunday school classes have likely had sexual intercourse.

There *is* good news in this survey, however. If 50 percent are involved in sex, the other 50 percent aren't. Some kids *are* making good decisions.

Today's young people need guidance. They need a healthy view of sex and sexuality. They need to move beyond simply saying yes to everything our culture says about sex and beyond simply saying no to their sexuality.

This 4-week course will help your senior highers openly and honestly explore their sexuality. It'll help them learn how to say yes to their God-given sexuality.

It'll also help them learn how to make responsible decisions about sex.

By the end of this course your students will:
● know the difference between sex and sexuality, and appreciate sexuality as more than just "plumbing;"
● identify our culture's view of sexuality and the biblical view;
● learn why the Christian faith approves sexual activity only in the context of the marriage relationship;
● learn that God's forgiveness is available for our mistakes—sexual or otherwise;
● identify dangers that go with a casual view of sex; and
● commit to making responsible sexual decisions.

COURSE OBJECTIVES

HOW TO USE THIS COURSE

ACTIVE LEARNING

Think back on an important lesson you've learned in life. Did you learn it from reading about it? from hearing about it? from something you experienced? Chances are, the most important lessons you've learned came from something you experienced. That's what active learning is—learning by doing. And active learning is a key element in Group's Active Bible Curriculum.

Active learning leads students in doing things that help them understand important principles, messages and ideas. It's a discovery process that helps kids internalize what they learn.

Each lesson section in Group's Active Bible Curriculum plays an important part in active learning:

The **Opener** involves kids in the topic in fun and unusual ways.

The **Action and Reflection** includes an experience designed to evoke specific feelings in the students. This section also processes those feelings through "How did you feel?" questions and applies the message to situations kids face.

The **Bible Application** actively connects the topic with the Bible. It helps kids see how the Bible is relevant to the situations they face.

The **Commitment** helps students internalize the Bible's message and commit to make changes in their lives.

The **Closing** funnels the lesson's message into a time of creative reflection and prayer.

When you put all the sections together, you get a lesson that's fun to teach—and kids get messages they'll remember.

BEFORE THE 4-WEEK SESSION

● Read the Introduction, the Course Objectives and This Course at a Glance.

● Decide how you'll publicize the course using the art on the Publicity Page (p. 9). Prepare fliers, newsletter articles and posters as needed.

● Look at the Bonus Ideas (p. 43) and decide which ones you'll use.

• Read the opening statements, Objectives and Bible Basis for the lesson. The Bible Basis shows how specific passages relate to senior highers today.

• Choose which Opener and Closing options to use. Each is appropriate for a different kind of group. The first option is often more active.

• Gather necessary supplies from This Lesson at a Glance.

• Read each section of the lesson. Adjust where necessary for your class size and meeting room.

• The approximate minutes listed give you an idea of how long each activity will take. Each lesson is designed to take 35 to 60 minutes. Shorten or lengthen activities as needed to fit your group.

• If you see you're going to have extra time, do an activity or two from the "If You Still Have Time . . ." box or from the Bonus Ideas (p. 43).

• Dive into the activities with the kids. Don't be a spectator. The lesson will be more successful and rewarding to both you and your students.

• The answers given after discussion questions are responses your students *might* give. They aren't the only answers or the "right" answers. If needed, use them to spark discussion. Kids won't always say what you wish they'd say. That's why some of the responses given are negative or controversial. If someone responds negatively, don't be shocked. Accept the person, and use the opportunity to explore other angles of the issue.

THIS COURSE AT A GLANCE

Before you dive into the lessons, familiarize yourself with each lesson aim. Then read the scripture passages.
● Study them as a background to the lessons.
● Use them as a basis for your personal devotions.
● Think about how they relate to teenagers' circumstances today.

LESSON 1: SEX AND SEXUALITY

Lesson Aim: To help senior highers understand and appreciate the difference between sex and sexuality.

Bible Basis: Genesis 1:26-28, 31; Genesis 2:18-25; and Song of Songs 1:1-3; 7:2-12.

LESSON 2: THE VIRTUES OF WAITING

Lesson Aim: To help senior highers understand why the Christian faith says to save sex for marriage.

Bible Basis: Matthew 22:34-40; Romans 6:12-20; and Ephesians 4:17—5:20.

LESSON 3: HOW TO SAY NO TO SEXUAL PRESSURE

Lesson Aim: To help senior highers learn how to resist sexual pressure.

Bible Basis: Romans 7:14-23; Romans 14:1-4, 22; and Ephesians 5:1-6.

LESSON 4: DANGERS OF PLAYING AROUND

Lesson Aim: To help senior highers understand the dangers and consequences associated with sex.

Bible Basis: Genesis 2:15-17 and Ezekiel 18:26-32.

PUBLICITY PAGE

Grab your senior highers' attention! Copy this page, then cut and paste the art of your choice in your church bulletin or newsletter to advertise this course on sexuality. Or copy and use the ready-made flier as a bulletin insert. Permission to photocopy this clip art is granted for local church use.

Splash this art on posters, fliers or even postcards! Just add the vital details: the date and time, and where you'll meet. It's that simple.

SEX: A Christian Perspective

SEX: A Christian Perspective

A 4-week high school course on sex and sexuality

Come to_____

On_____

At _____

Come learn what God has to say about our sexuality.

SEX AND SEXUALITY

Teenagers often confuse sexuality with sex; they reduce sexuality to the act of intercourse.
Yet there's a wonderful richness in God's gift of sexuality. Sexuality is more than just "plumbing" or the uniting of two bodies. At the heart of sexuality lies a relationship— the uniting of two people.

To help senior highers understand and appreciate the differences between sex and sexuality.

LESSON AIM

Students will:
- **identify how our culture views sexuality;**
- **explore what makes someone seem "sexy" to them;**
- **examine the differences between sex and sexuality;**
- **explore biblical affirmations of sexuality as a gift;**
- **affirm the gift of their own sexuality; and**
- **identify areas in which their views of sexuality need to grow.**

OBJECTIVES

Look up the following scriptures. Then read the background paragraphs to see how the passages relate to your senior highers.

In **Genesis 1:26-28, 31**, the writer describes God's gift of sex.

This passage reminds us that sex and sexuality are gifts from God and a part of God's plan for our lives. God considers sex to be a good part of his creation.

Many teenagers think God is somehow against sex. They forget that God invented sex. This passage serves as a reminder of the origin of our sexuality.

BIBLE BASIS
GENESIS 1:26-28, 31
GENESIS 2:18-25
SONG OF SONGS 1:1-3, 7:2-12

In **Genesis 2:18-25**, the writer describes the purpose of sex.

Sex is more than a way of reproducing. And it's more than a source of pleasure. This passage reminds us that the real purpose of sex is to bring a husband and wife into a relationship with each other—to bind two people together in oneness.

Senior highers need to understand that people of the opposite sex aren't objects to be taken advantage of. They need to see that sex is only meaningful in the context of a committed relationship—a marriage relationship.

In **Song of Songs 1:1-3; 7:2-12**, the writer describes the enjoyment of sex.

This passage vividly illustrates God's intent for sex. The writer joyfully describes the excitement and wonder of sexuality in the context of a marriage relationship.

Christian teenagers sometimes think the church always says no to sexual matters while our culture always says yes. This passage reminds them that the pleasures of sex are to be celebrated—in their proper context.

THIS LESSON AT A GLANCE

Section	Minutes	What Students Will Do	Supplies
Opener (Option 1)	5 to 10	**On the Radio**—Listen to popular songs about sex and discuss them.	Music cassettes, cassette player
(Option 2)		**The Bathroom Wall**—Talk about messages found on bathroom walls.	Tape, newsprint, markers
Action and Reflection	15 to 20	**Do You Think I'm Sexy?**—Determine what's sexy and discuss sexuality.	Fruit, rolls, orange juice, candy bars, pictures from magazines, photocopies of "Sexuality" box (p. 15)
Bible Application	10 to 15	**Male and Female**—Discuss the origin of sex and sexuality.	Bibles
Commitment	5 to 10	**And It Was Good**—Complete a handout and discuss the good and bad aspects of sexuality.	"And It Was Good" handout (p. 18), pencils
Closing (Option 1)	up to 5	**The Gift**—Say why they're thankful for their sexuality.	Wrapped gift
(Option 2)		**In God's Image**—Talk about what it means to be male or female.	Bible

The Lesson

☐ OPTION 1: ON THE RADIO

Arrange in advance for your class members to bring cassettes of current songs that express our culture's views of sex and sexuality. Get song recommendations from kids and bring some yourself in case kids forget.

Say: **We're surrounded by different views of sexuality. We're bombarded by sexual messages in television, songs, movies, magazines and on bathroom walls. Listen to the messages in current popular songs. Identify what each is saying about sex or sexuality.**

Play the songs one at a time. You'll only have time for a portion of each song. After each song segment, ask:

● **How does this song make you feel?** (Great; happy; upset.)

● **What does the song say about sex?** (Sex is wonderful; sex is dangerous; sex brings people closer together.)

● **How common is this view among your friends?** (It's very common; it's uncommon but not unknown; I've never heard this view expressed.)

● **Is this message healthy or unhealthy?** (Healthy, sex is a great thing; unhealthy, sex outside of marriage is wrong.)

Repeat this process with portions of at least three songs, then ask:

● **What do television, songs, movies and magazines say about sex and sexuality?** (Sex is fun; casual sex is okay; what I do isn't anybody else's business; sex is dangerous.)

Say: **Today we're going to dive into a touchy subject— sex. We'll begin to understand the difference between the picture of sex portrayed by our culture and sexuality according to its creator—God.**

☐ OPTION 2: THE BATHROOM WALL

Tape a sheet of newsprint to the wall. Write the word "Sex" across the top of the sheet.

Ask:

● **How many of you have read what's written on bathroom walls at school?**

● **Without using the actual words, what's written there?** (Who's having sex with who; telephone numbers; graphic pictures.)

Say: **On the wall we have a large sheet of newsprint with the word "sex" written on it. We're going to create our own bathroom-wall graffiti. But instead of resorting to pictures and four-letter words, we'll write what our society says to us about sex and sexuality. Think of all the** messages you've heard—in television, music, movies and magazines. Choose one or two messages and write them on our "bathroom wall." You may want to use song lyrics, phrases from commercials or anything else you've heard.

Give teenagers each a marker. Allow them a few minutes to write, then ask:

● **According to the "bathroom wall" we've created, what does our culture say about sex and sexuality?** (Sex is dirty; sex is fun; if it feels good, do it.)

● **Do your friends agree or disagree with this message? Explain.** (Agree, they think sex is cool; disagree, they believe sex is wrong outside of marriage.)

● **Is this message healthy, unhealthy or both? Explain.** (Just saying no is healthy; portraying sex as something "just for fun" is unhealthy.)

Say: **You've all heard other people's opinions on sex and sexuality. Today we're going right to the creator of sex—God—to uncover a Christian perspective on sex and sexuality.**

ACTION AND REFLECTION
(15 to 20 minutes)

DO YOU THINK I'M SEXY?

Cut out pictures of people from a variety of magazines. Include pictures of young and old, male and female, fully clothed and partially clothed people (people wearing bathing suits). Be sure some of the pictures are of stereotypical people who might be considered sexy by your kids, and some that might not be considered sexy. Have at least twice as many pictures as there are people in your class.

Also, in another room have a breakfast of fruit, rolls and orange juice prepared and waiting for kids. Don't tell kids about the breakfast. Give each kid a snack-size candy bar. Tell them each to eat their candy bar right away.

Say: **For the next few minutes we'll be talking about what it means to be sexy and what makes a person sexually desirable. This wall represents "ultra-sexy."** (Point to a wall.) **This wall represents "zero sex-appeal."** (Point to the wall opposite the first one.) **Take a few seconds to look at the magazine pictures. Choose a picture. Then stand between the two extremes where you feel the person in the picture best fits.**

Have class members each hold up their picture so everyone can see it and explain why they rated it as they did.

Ask:

● **Would anyone like to move another person's picture to a different place between the extremes?**

If any teenagers answer yes, have them explain where they'd place a picture and why they disagree with the person who originally placed it.

Form a circle and ask:

● **What makes someone seem sexy?** (A good body; nice smile; clothes he or she wears.)

● **Why did we disagree on some of the pictures?** (People have different tastes; some people like to look at bodies, others like to look at faces.)

Say: **Before we go any further with our lesson, I have a surprise for you.**

Get the breakfast food from the other room, and bring it into the class. Watch kids' reactions as they see the food.

Ask:

● **How do you feel about being served breakfast this morning?** (Great; it was a good idea; I'm hungry.)

● **How do you feel about having eaten your dessert first?** (I should've waited; I wish I hadn't eaten it; it doesn't bother me.)

● **How is a candy bar or other dessert item like sex?** (It tastes good; it should be saved until after a meal just as sex should be saved until after marriage; it's fun but not necessarily healthy.)

● **How would you define "sexuality"?** (Gender; sexual attraction; sexual intercourse.)

Say: **Just as the candy bar was only one part of a larger meal, sex is one part of our sexuality. The candy bar may taste great, but it alone won't give you the nourishment you need to be healthy. Similarly, sex alone won't create healthy relationships. And as we'll learn in a later lesson, sex before marriage can hinder your enjoyment of your spouse's sexuality.**

Sometimes people confuse sex with sexuality, which is a much broader topic. The word "sex" has two different meanings. It can refer to our gender—our sex is either male or female. Or it can refer to the sex act—intercourse. Sexuality includes an even wider perspective of who we are.

Form groups of no more than five. Distribute copies of the "Sexuality" box to each group. Have groups each briefly discuss the questions in the box.

Form a circle and ask:

● **How did you feel talking about sexuality?** (Embarrassed; fine; uncomfortable.)

● **Which items on this list helped you decide how to rate the pictures?** (Sexual values; sexual orientation.)

Say: **Sexuality is more than simply having sex. God created us as sexual beings. And it's important to understand our sexuality according to God's perspective.**

Sexuality

Read the following descriptions of sexuality. Then discuss the questions at the end.

Our sexuality includes:

1. Sexual Identity—what it means to be male or female.

2. Sexual Roles—how we relate to members of our sex and the opposite sex. This includes our understanding of what it means to be masculine or feminine.

3. Sexual Orientation—who we're attracted to.

4. Sexual Behavior—how we express our sexuality in relationships with both sexes.

5. Sexual Values—what we believe is right and wrong, acceptable and unacceptable, permitted and not permitted. This also includes what we think is sexy and what we think isn't.

● Do you agree with these statements? Why or why not?

● Which of these items is easiest to talk about? most difficult? Explain.

● How do you feel about your own sexuality?

MALE AND FEMALE

Say: **Sometimes we forget, but God is the one who created sex and gave us the gift of our sexuality. Although the Bible is full of warnings about abuses of sexuality, it also has a positive view of sexuality. Let's look at some examples.**

Form groups of no more than six. Give groups each a Bible and assign them each one of the following passages: Genesis 2:18-25; Genesis 2:26-28, 31; and Song of Songs 1:1-3; 7:2-12. Make sure all three passages are assigned.

Have groups each designate a reporter to share the results of their discussion with the whole group. Have groups each read their passage and answer the following questions:

● **What does this passage say about sex or sexuality?**
● **What's the purpose of sexuality in this passage?**

After the discussion, have the reporters each read their passage aloud to the class and summarize their group's answers.

Then ask:

● **Taken together, what do these passages say about sex and sexuality?** (Sex is good in the right circumstance; sex can be wonderful.)

● **Does this surprise you? Why or why not?** (Yes, I thought the Bible taught that sex was dirty; no, I knew God created sex for us to enjoy in marriage.)

AND IT WAS GOOD

Give each class member a photocopy of the "And It Was Good" handout (p. 18) and a pencil. Have them each complete the handout by writing in the appropriate outline (according to their sex) answers to the questions at the top of the page.

Form a circle, and have kids each share what they wrote on their handout. Then have kids each take a turn standing in the center of the circle while others call out specific characteristics they appreciate about them. Be sure everyone gets a chance to be in the circle. Some kids may feel uncomfortable standing in the circle, but encourage them to participate anyway. This exercise helps kids see God made them "and they are good."

Table Talk

The Table Talk activity in this course helps senior highers talk with their parents about sex and sexuality.

If you choose to use the Table Talk activity, this is a good time to show students the "Table Talk" handout (p. 19). Ask them each to spend time with their parents completing it.

Before kids leave, give them each the "Table Talk" handout to take home, or tell them you'll send it to their parents.

Or use the Table Talk idea found in the Bonus Ideas (p. 44) for a meeting based on the handout.

☐ OPTION 1: THE GIFT

Place a wrapped gift in the center of the circle.

Say: **This package symbolizes the gift of sexuality God has given each of us. As the package comes to you, share one reason you're thankful for this gift. Then pass the gift to the next person.**

Begin with yourself, saying something such as, "I'm thankful for this gift because it makes me who I am" or "I'm thankful for this gift because it's something to enjoy in marriage." Then pass the package to the person on your left. Set the tone for sharing, and remind kids to be serious during this time. When the package returns to you, close with a prayer thanking God for each teenager and his or her gift of sexuality.

☐ OPTION 2: IN GOD'S IMAGE

Read aloud Genesis 1:27. Beginning with yourself, have each person share what it means personally to be male or female. Encourage kids to be serious and say something positive about their sexual identity, such as "I'm glad to be a guy because I enjoy sports" or "I'm glad to be a girl because I enjoy fun clothes." After each person shares, have the whole class say in unison "Thank you, Lord, for the gift of our sexuality."

CLOSING
(up to 5 minutes)

If You Still Have Time . . .

Affirmation of Sexuality—Form groups of no more than five. Have each group write a one-paragraph affirmation of God's gift of sexuality. Have the paragraphs begin with "We believe . . . " Then have groups each share what they've written.

Scripture Paraphrase—Form groups of no more than five. Have groups each create a song or pantomime using one of the Genesis passages from Male and Female. Have groups each share what they've written.

And It Was Good

Write your completion of the following sentences inside the appropriate box. If you're a guy, write in the guy box; if you're a girl, write in the girl box.

1. One thing about my sexuality I thank God for is . . .
2. One thing I think God's concerned about in our culture's view of sexuality is . . .
3. One thing I can do to develop a healthy Christian perspective of sex and sexuality is . . .

1.

2.

3.

1.

2.

3.

Table Talk

Dear Parent: We're involved in a senior high course at church called, "Sex: A Christian Perspective." Students are learning about God's intent for sex and our sexuality. We'd like you and your teenager to spend some time discussing this important topic. Use this "Table Talk" page to help you.

Complete the following sentences:

Parent:
- My first crush or love was . . .
- One thing I liked about the physical appearance of a member of the opposite sex was . . .
- My most embarrassing moment on a date was . . .
- I learned my sexual values from . . .
- I decided how far to go sexually after . . .
- Talking about sex makes me feel . . .
- I believe God created sexuality for . . .

Senior Higher:
- My first crush or love was . . .
- What I like in the physical appearance of a member of the opposite sex is . . .
- My most embarrassing moment on a date was . . . (If you haven't had one, describe what would embarrass you.)
- I learned my sexual values from . . .
- In order to decide how far to go sexually, I will . . .
- Talking about sex makes me feel . . .
- I believe God created sexuality for . . .

Talk Topics

Discuss the "Talk Topics" with each other. Use the following format for each topic.
1. The senior higher shares without the parent interrupting or making any comment.
2. The parent shares without the senior higher interrupting or making any comment.
3. Both parent and senior higher ask each other questions for clarification, but still don't respond to what's said.
4. Both parent and senior higher respond to what's said.
5. Both parent and senior higher talk openly about the topic, each sharing thoughts and feelings.

- Fears I have in talking to you about sex
- What I need from you as we talk about sex
- What I think you already know about my sexuality
- What you need to know about my sexuality
- For me sex is . . .
- Premarital sex

- Birth control
- Sexually transmitted diseases
- Teenage pregnancy
- Making out
- Masturbation

Read aloud Genesis 1:26-31. Talk about what's good about the gift of sexuality.

LESSON 2

THE VIRTUES OF WAITING

Today's kids are under many sexual pressures. Everything in our society seems to scream "do it!" Magazines, movies, TV shows, songs and peers say: "It's okay to have sex with someone you love." So why should teenagers fight against these pressures in order to keep their virginity? Kids need answers to that question.

LESSON AIM

To help senior highers understand why the Christian faith says to save sex for marriage.

OBJECTIVES

Students will:
- explore why sex should be saved for marriage;
- learn what "love" means; and
- hear of God's forgiveness for people who make sexual mistakes.

BIBLE BASIS

MATTHEW 22:34-40
ROMANS 6:12-20
EPHESIANS 4:17-5:20

Look up the following scriptures. Then read the background paragraphs to see how the passages relate to your senior highers.

In **Matthew 22:34-40**, Jesus describes the greatest commandments.

Jesus makes it clear in this passage what's behind all the "do's" and "don'ts" in the Bible. He's concerned about the quality of our relationships and our ability to express love. This passage clearly shows the importance of love in any relationship.

Senior highers can learn from this passage that the quality of a relationship may be measured by how much love we have for the other person. They can learn that love, not sex, is the key to vital and fulfilling relationships.

In **Romans 6:12-20**, Paul describes how to offer our bodies to God as instruments of righteousness.

What does it mean to be an instrument of righteousness? Paul suggests it involves allowing God to direct the actions of our bodies and the thoughts of our minds. He encourages readers to avoid following the desires of the body.

Senior highers naturally have strong physical desires for sexual intimacy. This passage details the importance of letting God help them overcome sexual temptations.

In **Ephesians 4:17-5:20**, Paul describes the morality and lifestyle changes that follow becoming a Christian.

As Christians, our love for God and for others is expressed in all we do. All parts of our lives, including our sexuality, must express who we are as God's people.

Senior highers need to understand that they can't just "have sex" without involving the whole person. This passage can help them see how to bring all of their actions and choices into alignment with their faith.

THIS LESSON AT A GLANCE

Section	Minutes	What Students Will Do	Supplies
Opener (Option 1)	5 to 10	**The Last Virgin**—Determine reasons for losing or keeping virginity.	Paper, pencils
(Option 2)		**The Insurance Policy**—Brainstorm things that make up a secure relationship.	Newsprint, marker, tape
Action and Reflection	10 to 15	**The Fruits of Love**—Talk about the pros and cons of saving sex for marriage.	Fruit (apples or peaches), newspapers
Bible Application	10 to 15	**Why Should God Care?**—Examine what God says about sex and relationships.	Bibles
Commitment	10 to 15	**More Than a Feeling**—Complete a handout and compare love with lust.	"Love, Infatuation or Lust?" handout (p. 27), pencils, Bible
Closing (Option 1)	up to 5	**Caring Is Forgiving**—Experience how it feels to be forgiven.	
(Option 2)		**Support Systems**—Experience how they can support one another.	Unbruised fruit from The Fruits of Love

The Lesson

☐ OPTION 1: THE LAST VIRGIN

Form groups of no more than four. Give groups each a sheet of paper and a pencil.

Say: **Jenny feels like the last virgin in the world. It seems most of her friends have already had sex. Jenny feels she just wants to get "it" over with. But she also thinks it's best to wait until she's married.**

Jenny's confused and has come to you for advice. Her problem involves very deep feelings. She's asked you what she should do.

In your groups, decide how you'll respond to Jenny about her concerns. You may choose to advise her to have sex or to wait. You don't have to agree with the advice your group gives. Write your group's response and reasoning on the paper.

After a few minutes, have groups each read aloud their response to Jenny's problem.

For each response, ask:

● **How do you feel about this response?** (Glad; sad; indifferent.)

● **Why would you give Jenny this advice?** (It's what I'd do; it's what God would want; she's too young; she's old enough.)

● **How would you react if you were Jenny and someone gave you this advice?** (I'd be upset; I'd feel relieved; I'd be more confused.)

Say: **The decision to have or not have sex before marriage is an important one. It's not to be taken lightly. People have all kinds of advice about it, but today we'll take a look at what God—the creator of our sexuality—has to say about the virtues of waiting.**

☐ OPTION 2: THE INSURANCE POLICY

Say: **Today we're going to create a relationship insurance policy that would guarantee your emotional, spiritual and physical safety in intimate, romantic relationships.**

Tape two sheets of newsprint to a wall. Have the class members brainstorm things they'd want from another person to feel safe in the relationship. For example: trust, love and commitment. Write these on one sheet of newsprint.

Next, have the class brainstorm things they'd be willing to give to make the relationship safe. List these on the other sheet of newsprint.

Ask:
- **Is anything missing? If so, what?**
- **How would you feel in a relationship consisting of the attributes listed on the newsprint?** (Safe; loved.)
- **What would bring about this kind of relationship?** (Knowing the other person really loved me; knowing each other for a long time; marriage; nothing.)
- **How is the relationship we described like marriage?** (Real marriages aren't that way; it's too idealistic; it's just like marriage should be.)
- **How is a marriage commitment such as the one we've described like an insurance policy?** (It insures the commitment; it isn't.)

Say: **In a God-directed marriage commitment, you've got a stable insurance policy. But sexual attraction alone is a pretty weak insurance policy for a relationship. Today, we're going to explore why the Bible advises us to save sex for marriage.**

Table Talk Follow-Up

If you sent the "Table Talk" handout (p. 19) to parents last week, discuss students' reactions to the activity. Ask volunteers to share what they learned from the discussion with their parents.

THE FRUITS OF LOVE

In a room with an uncarpeted, hard floor, form groups of no more than four. If your room is carpeted, place newspapers over the carpeting. Give groups each two pieces of fruit—apples or firm peaches work best. Have groups each stand, form a circle and place one piece of fruit in the center of the circle. Have someone in each group hold the other piece of fruit.

Say: **In your groups, talk about the pros and cons of having sex before marriage. Also, talk about how the media portrays sex. As you talk, toss one piece of fruit around your circle. Whenever you hear a pro for having sex before marriage, drop the fruit, then pick it up and begin again. You'll have four minutes to discuss your feelings about the subject.**

On "go," have groups begin discussing and tossing the fruit. Go around to each group and help keep the conversations going. After four minutes, call time. Have kids remain in their circles and sit down. Then have them pass around bruised and non-bruised fruit for everyone to inspect.

Ask:
- **How does the piece of fruit you've been tossing around look?** (Ugly; bruised; gross.)
- **By comparison, how does the fruit that remained in**

ACTION AND REFLECTION
(10 to 15 minutes)

the center of the circle look? (Much better; more appetizing.)

● **Which piece of fruit would you rather eat? Which would you rather be? Explain.**

● **How is someone who has sex before marriage like the bruised fruit?** (He or she might feel used; he or she might have emotional bruises just as the fruit has bruises.)

Say: **The potential negative aspects of sex before marriage aren't always as obvious as the bruises on the fruit. Sometimes they're well-hidden and may not appear until after that person is married. God created sex as a beautiful expression of two people's love for each other. And he created the marriage relationship as the context for sex.**

Ask:

● **How do you think God feels when his followers choose to save sex until marriage?** (Happy; thrilled; pleased.)

Say: **God smiles on our decisions to follow his Word. And when we make mistakes, he has the power to renew us so we can begin again to do his will. Next we'll take a look at how we can follow his will and accept his forgiveness.**

BIBLE APPLICATION
(10 to 15 minutes)

WHY SHOULD GOD CARE?

Ask:

● **Why should God care if we have sex or not?** (Because God loves us; it's not God's business; God doesn't want us to have fun; God doesn't want us to be hurt.)

Say: **The Christian faith has always placed sex in the context of the marriage relationship. We're going to look at some scripture passages to help us understand why.**

Form groups of no more than six. Give groups each a Bible and assign one of the following passages: Matthew 22:34-40; Romans 6:12-20; and Ephesians 4:17—5:20. Make sure all three passages are assigned.

Have groups each read their passage and be prepared to answer the following questions:

● **What's the concern expressed in this passage?**
● **Why is it important?**
● **How does it relate to having or not having sex?**

Have groups each present the message of their passage to the other groups as if they were talking to their own teenage sons and daughters.

Say: **God cares about us and wants what's best for us. God wants us to have healthy, supportive relationships—and to save sex for marriage. But some people argue that "being in love" is a good enough reason to have sex. Let's think about what that argument is all about.**

COMMITMENT
(10 to 15 minutes)

MORE THAN A FEELING

Ask the class to evaluate if being "in love" with someone is a good reason for having sex with that person.

Say: **When we use the word "love," we're usually refer-ring to a feeling. We fall in love with someone. And, often just as quickly, we fall out of love. Our culture defines love as a feeling.**

The Bible has a fundamentally different view of love. For God, love is not a feeling. It's a commitment to the well-being of another. Love is a decision to treat another person in a particular way and to live out that decision—regardless of what our feelings are that moment. Using the Bible's definition, it's possible to love someone even when you don't like him or her.

Have someone read aloud 1 Corinthians 13.

Ask:

● **How is this definition of love different from our cul-ture's?** (This is selfless love, our culture defines love as what we can get; this love is more giving.)

Distribute "Love, Infatuation or Lust?" handouts (p. 27) and pencils to students. Have teenagers each complete the handout. Then form groups of no more than four. Have groups each discuss the completed handouts. After a few minutes, form a circle.

Ask:

● **What's the difference between love and lust?** (Love is more than a feeling; lust is purely physical attraction, love is more than sex.)

● **How can having sex hurt another person?** (They could become emotionally scarred; they could feel guilty.)

Read aloud John 8:1-11.

● **Many people have fallen into the temptation to follow lust instead of love. According to this passage, how does Jesus respond to those people?** (You're forgiven; avoid this sin from now on; I love you anyway.)

Ask teenagers each to close their eyes and silently commit to saving sex for marriage. Also, urge them to ask God's for-giveness for any sexual mistakes they may've already made.

☐ OPTION 1: CARING IS FORGIVING

Have the teenagers stand in a circle with their arms around each other.

Say: **For this exercise I'll make a statement and ask you to do something. Silently do what I say to do.**

● **If you've ever been insensitive to the feelings of a member of the opposite sex . . . close your eyes and keep them closed.**

● **If you've ever been hurt by a member of the opposite sex due to his or her insensitivity . . . drop your arms.**

● **If you've ever been more interested in yourself than in the other person in a relationship . . . turn around and face away from the circle.**

● **If you've ever hurt another person . . . sit down.**

● **If you've ever felt used in a relationship . . . scoot**

C L O S I N G
(up to 5 minutes)

away from the circle a foot or two.

● In the Bible, the Apostle Paul says: "All have sinned and fallen short of the glory of God." All of us have been hurt. All of us have hurt others. That's why God is so concerned about our whole being—including our sexuality.

● If you can forgive those who've hurt you . . . stand up.

● If you hope you'll be forgiven for any hurt you may have caused someone . . . turn around and face inward.

● If you think people aren't things to be used . . . walk forward and form a tight circle again.

● If you think people's feelings are important . . . open your eyes.

● If you're willing to ask for God's help as you make sexual decisions . . . link arms.

Close with a prayer asking God to help teenagers make responsible sex decisions, forgive their mistakes and live as God would have them live.

☐ OPTION 2: SUPPORT SYSTEMS

Have the group form a circle facing in and stand hip to hip. Then have everyone turn 90 degrees to the right. Then have kids each put their hands on the shoulders of the person in front of them and sit on the lap of the person behind them.

While everyone is supporting each other, ask:

● **What's it like supporting and being supported by each other?** (It's a great feeling; it's comforting.)

If this exercise doesn't work, use this opportunity to discuss what happens when kids don't support each other.

Say: **God wants this feeling of comfort and security for us in all of our relationships—especially in marriage. And just as we can support each other in this circle, we can help each other save sex until marriage.**

Pass one of the unbruised pieces of fruit from The Fruits of Love activity around the circle. As teenagers each pass the fruit to the next person, have them say "With God's help, you can wait and save sex for marriage" to that person. Close with a brief group prayer thanking God for caring about the kind of relationships Christians have.

If You Still Have Time . . .

Guilty Feelings—Have teenagers brainstorm sexual situations or behaviors that could make someone feel guilty. Role-play helping a friend who feels guilty about sexual behavior.

Virginity's Virtues—Form two groups with guys in one, girls in the other. Have each group make a list of the positive reasons a person of the opposite sex should remain a virgin, or ask forgiveness and refrain from having further sex. Bring the groups together. Have the girls tell what they came up with while the guys sit quietly and listen. Then have the guys respond to what they heard. Repeat the process with the guys talking and the girls listening and responding.

LOVE, INFATUATION OR LUST?

Read the situations below. Write "lust," "infatuation" or "love" next to each situation. Use these definitions:

- **Lust** is physical or sexual attraction.
- **Infatuation** is being crazy about a person, but the relationship is dependent on your feelings.
- **Love** is a commitment to that person and a decision to place his or her needs equal to or above your own.

_____ This person is so attractive that you just want to stare at him or her.

_____ Your whole body tingles when this person touches you.

_____ This person doesn't ever ask how you're feeling or seem to care about your needs, but you don't mind because he or she is so popular and attractive.

_____ You can talk to this person for hours about anything.

_____ This person is your best friend. He or she just happens to be of the opposite sex.

_____ You feel like you have to look and act your best around this person. You don't ever want him or her to see the real you.

_____ This person worships the ground you walk on. He or she is willing to make any compromise.

_____ This person only needs a few changes to be perfect. You're determined to change him or her.

_____ This person has some qualities that bother you, but you can put up with them because they're not really important.

_____ You share a lot of common interests and values with this person.

LESSON 3

HOW TO SAY NO TO SEXUAL PRESSURE

Half of America's teenagers are saying no to sex. But what about the other half? The ability to make responsible decisions can be taught and learned. Even kids who've been sexually active can stop.

In a culture that glamorizes sex, we need to teach our young people how to be responsible and avoid sexual pressure—and we need to give them support for their decision.

LESSON AIM

To help senior highers learn how to resist sexual pressure.

OBJECTIVES

Students will:
● evaluate and discuss various pressure situations and techniques;
● practice saying no in a non-threatening environment; and
● explore the Bible's view of inner struggle.

BIBLE BASIS

ROMANS 7:14-23
ROMANS 14:1-4, 22
EPHESIANS 5:1-6

Look up the following scriptures. Then read the background paragraphs to see how the passages relate to your senior highers.

In **Romans 7:14-23**, Paul describes his inner struggles.

In this familiar passage, Paul lets us know that being a Christian wasn't easy for him. He knew what God wanted for his life, but he found it hard to make his behavior match what he knew to be God's will.

Teenagers can readily identify with Paul's struggle. By the time they reach senior high, most have learned what's "wrong" and "right" according to the Bible's teaching. But like Paul, they often have trouble doing what they know God wants.

In **Romans 14:1-4, 22**, Paul reminds us not to judge one another's opinions.

Once we know what God's will is for our lives, we need to grab hold of that knowledge and turn it into practice. In this passage, Paul simply argues that knowing what's right isn't enough. We also need to act aggressively on our convictions.

As senior highers become adults, they learn integrity—the ability to stand firm on what they believe, even in the face of pressure to give in. When teenagers are tempted or pressured to give in to sexual desires they know are wrong, they can follow Paul's advice and hold fast to what's right.

In **Ephesians 5:1-6**, Paul warns us not to be deceived.

Paul didn't want Christians to be like everyone else. In this passage, Paul reminds the early Christians not to be taken in by false teachings but to discover what God wants for their lives.

Teenagers hear many voices telling them what to do and be. But as Paul encourages in this passage, teenagers can learn to hear God's voice above all the others—and act on God's will.

THIS LESSON AT A GLANCE

Section	Minutes	What Students Will Do	Supplies
Opener (Option 1)	5 to 10	**If You Loved Me . . .**—Play a game and experience pressure to do something they don't want to do.	Chairs
(Option 2)		**Sexual Pressure Meter**—Write situations where kids might be under sexual pressure.	3×5 cards, pencils, tape
Action and Reflection	10 to 15	**Just Say No**—Role-play what it's like to say no to pressure.	Chairs, tape, newsprint, markers
Bible Application	10 to 15	**Hold Fast**—Discuss what the Bible says about making good sexual decisions.	Bibles, pipe cleaners
Commitment	10 to 15	**How to Say No**—Write letters to help teenagers deal with sexual pressures.	"Letters From Paul" handout (p. 34), pencils
Closing (Option 1)	up to 5	**Big Brother, Big Sister**—Commit to help each other say no to sexual pressures.	Pipe cleaner structures from Hold Fast
(Option 2)		**Opposite Sex**—Discuss reasons to respect a no to sexual pressure.	

The Lesson

☐ OPTION 1: IF YOU LOVED ME . . .

Have teenagers sit in a circle. Say: **The object of our opening game is to "seduce" another person and make him or her give in to you by smiling. The person being pressured should resist and try not to smile.**

Explain the following rules to the class.

1. The seducer must sit in another person's lap and say, "If you loved me, you would."

2. The seducer can beg, plead, play with the person's hair or whatever. But the seducer can't tickle.

3. The seducer may repeat the line up to three times. After each time the seducer says "If you loved me, you would," the intended "victim" must say "I love you, but I won't smile" without smiling or laughing.

4. If the victim smiles or laughs, he or she becomes the seducer and the process repeats itself with a new temptee.

5. If the victim successfully resists, the seducer moves on to a new person. After two unsuccessful attempts, a new seducer and victim are chosen.

Play the game for five minutes, then ask:

● **What was it like being the seducer?** (Fun; challenging; embarrassing.)

● **Was it easy or difficult to avoid the temptation to smile? Explain.** (Easy, I wasn't in a smiling mood; difficult, the seducer was too funny.)

Say: **Just as some of you had a tough time keeping a straight face in this game, many teenagers have a difficult time saying no to the pressure to have sex. Today we're going to be talking about how to say no to sexual pressures.**

☐ OPTION 2: SEXUAL PRESSURE METER

Distribute 3×5 cards and pencils. Have class members write situations where a teenager might be under sexual pressure, such as: going to a party where couples begin to pair off; going on a date to a steamy movie; watching television at home alone with a date.

Designate one wall as a Sexual Pressure Meter. Explain that the top of the wall represents "Too Hot to Handle" and the bottom of the wall represents "No Pressure at All." Have kids each read their card aloud then tape it to the wall at a height that represents how much sexual pressure the situation would put on them.

After all cards have been placed, ask:

● **Do you agree with the placement of these cards? Why**

or why not?

If kids disagree with any card's placement, have the group discuss the situation.

● **What does the way our group has positioned the cards tell you?**

● **What makes it easy or hard to resist sexual pressure?** (It's difficult to control your desires; I keep telling myself it's best to wait and that makes it easier.)

Say: **For some people, all the cards you created might be at the bottom of the wall. But for many others, the sexual pressures they feel would place them near the ceiling. Almost everyone feels some kind of sexual pressure at one time or another. Today we'll examine how we can respond to that pressure with a confident no.**

JUST SAY NO

Form pairs. Have guys pair up with girls as much as possible. Have partners sit in chairs facing each other. Have pairs each determine who'll be #1 and who'll be #2.

Have #1s each plead with #2s to switch chairs with them. Tell #1s to beg, plead, threaten, bribe or use any other method to convince #2s to switch.

Tell #2s not to give in to #1s' request.

Do this for two minutes, and then have partners switch numbers and repeat the process.

Form a circle, and ask:

● **How hard was it to say no?** (Not too hard; easy; difficult as time went on.)

● **How did you feel when you were pressured?** (Uncomfortable; strong.)

● **How is this situation like being pressured to have sex?** (The pressure was strong; people tried all sorts of tactics.)

● **Did you ever want to give in and do what the #1s requested? Why or why not?** (Yes, I was tired of hearing him or her beg; no, I knew I should stand my ground.)

Tape two sheets of newsprint to the wall. Write "Tactics" on one and "How to Say No" on the other. Ask kids to call out tactics #1s used to try to convince #2s to change seats. List these on the "Tactics" newsprint. Then have kids describe techniques #2s used to avoid giving in. List these on the "How to Say No" newsprint.

Have kids reword each "Tactic" and "How to Say No" response in terms of pressure to have sex. Discuss each of these briefly.

Then ask:

● **Which tactic listed on the newsprint is the toughest to say no to? Explain.**

● **Why do people give in and do things they don't really want to do?** (Because they're weak; they don't really know what they want; they want to make other people happy.)

Say: **Even Bible characters struggled with giving in and**

doing things they didn't want to do. Next, we'll look at Paul's struggle and methods for dealing with that struggle.

HOLD FAST

Form groups of no more than four. Have someone read aloud Romans 7:14-23 to the whole class.

Ask:

● **Have you ever felt like Paul did in this passage? If yes, describe that time.**

Assign one of the following passages to each group: Romans 14:1-4, 22 or Ephesians 5:1-6.

Give groups each a supply of pipe cleaners. Have groups each sculpt a symbol representing the message of their passage as it relates to overcoming sexual pressure. For example, a group might sculpt a person facing away from the word "sex" to illustrate Paul's advice to avoid sexual impurity. Have groups each explain their sculpture to the rest of the class.

Then ask:

● **In Ephesians 5:1-6, sexual impurity is only one item among many mentioned. How would this passage, as a whole, help us in making sexual decisions?** (We should get our lives in order and avoid temptations; we should choose only good things to think about.)

● **How might Paul's guidance in these scriptures help you resist sexual pressure?** (It reminds me to seek God first; pressure is inevitable, I just need to work hard to avoid it.)

Say: **Like Paul, we struggle to do what God wants—and sometimes fail. But also like Paul, we can use our knowledge and strength to help others overcome sexual pressures.**

HOW TO SAY NO

Say: **Imagine you're the Apostle Paul and you have a chance to counsel a teenager who's constantly tempted by sexual pressures. How would you counsel that teenager? What would you say?**

Give each teenager a "Letters From Paul" handout (p. 34) and a pencil. Have kids each complete the handout and silently answer the questions at the bottom of the sheet.

After kids finish, form pairs. Have partners talk briefly about their handouts.

Then ask the whole group:

● **Were the letters easy or difficult to answer? Explain.** (Easy, the answers were obvious to me; difficult, I'm not sure I know what's right.)

● **Would God have answered them the same way you did? Why or why not?**

Then say: **One of the best ways we can learn to avoid**

sexual pressure is to support each other's decision to say no. In your pairs, take a few seconds to say two or three things you appreciate about your partner that will help him or her to be strong in difficult situations. Begin by saying: "Sometimes it's tough, but I know you can overcome sexual pressure by ..."

For example, kids might complete the phrase by saying, "avoiding tempting situations" or "asking for God's help." Some kids may want to joke around because they feel uncomfortable talking about such a personal subject. Remind them that God wants us to be supportive of each other; we need to be serious because no one knows the personal struggles someone else might be going through.

☐ OPTION 1: BIG BROTHER, BIG SISTER

Have partners each commit to being each other's "big brother" or "big sister" during the coming weeks. Encourage them to be accountable to one another about tough situations they face.

Form a circle. Place the pipe-cleaner sculptures from Hold Fast in the center of the circle. Say: **As we face sexual pressure situations, let's remember Paul's advice and learn to say no when we know something's wrong.**

Close with prayer. Then have kids each take part of a pipe-cleaner sculpture home with them as a reminder to follow Paul's advice and say no to sexual pressure.

☐ OPTION 2: OPPOSITE SEX

Form pairs. Have guys pair up with girls as much as possible. Have one person in each pair interview the other for one to two minutes on why a no from a member of the opposite sex should be respected. Reverse roles and repeat the process.

Have the class form a circle. Then close with a circle prayer in which kids each thank God for one thing they appreciate about what their partner said.

CLOSING
(up to 5 minutes)

If You Still Have Time ...

Dating Guide—Have groups of no more than five write a "Dating Guide" for kids in the church who'll soon be dating. Have them include how to avoid or resist sexual pressure.

Peer Pressure Reversal Committee—Have kids brainstorm practical ways to tell their friends at school how to avoid sexual pressures. Form groups of no more than four, and have each group develop one of the brainstormed ideas so it could actually be implemented. Have kids pick one or two of the ideas and put them into action.

Letters from Paul

If you were the Apostle Paul, how would you respond to the following letters from Christian teenagers? Write your answers in the space provided. Then silently answer the questions at the bottom of the page.

Dear Paul,
  I'm in love. I'm 16 and my girlfriend is 17. We've been dating for about five months. Lately, we've been getting closer physically, and I'm not sure what we're doing is right. We haven't had sex—yet—but I know we'll have to make that decision soon. We really love each other. Would having sex be wrong?
          Sincerely,
          Unsure

Dear Unsure,

Dear Paul,
  When I was 16, I had sex with a guy I knew from school. I felt guilty afterward, but I think I've forgiven myself for my mistake. My problem now is everyone thinks I'm "easy." The guys I date want me to go to bed with them, and some of my girlfriends tease me about being "experienced." I don't want to make the same mistake twice, but everyone I go out with pressures me to have sex. What can I do?
          Sincerely,
          Paying for
          my mistake

Dear Paying,

● If you could ask Paul for advice on a sexual question, what would you ask?
● How would Jesus want you to act in a situation similar to either of the two recorded above?
● How will the decisions you make as a teenager affect your future?

DANGERS OF PLAYING AROUND

S ex can be one of the most fulfilling gifts God has given us. And it can also be the source of incredible harm.

Senior highers often think, "It can't happen to me!" They feel invincible. But they aren't. Teenagers get pregnant. Teenagers catch sexually transmitted diseases. Teenagers make wrong decisions with consequences that affect the rest of their lives.

To help senior highers understand the dangers and consequences associated with sex.

LESSON AIM

Students will:
● take a test to see how much they know about the dangers of sex;
● explore what the Bible says about consequences and responsibility;
● discuss ways to deal with the consequences of sexual behavior; and
● commit to making responsible sexual decisions.

OBJECTIVES

Look up the following scriptures. Then read the background paragraphs to see how the passages relate to your senior highers.

In **Genesis 2:15-17**, God sets limits for Adam in the Garden of Eden.

One of the hardest lessons in life is that we can't do anything we want without the possibility of suffering the conse-

BIBLE BASIS
GENESIS 2:15-17
EZEKIEL 18:26-32

quences. From the beginning, God placed limits on what we could do—for our own good. Some things are too dangerous—they may even lead to death.

Senior highers often have a limited perspective on consequences. As they consciously develop their independence, they may have a hard time accepting limits to their freedom. They need to see—as Adam and Eve did— that actions may prompt unavoidable and often negative consequences.

In **Ezekiel 18:26-32**, the author describes how we're responsible for our own actions.

This message updates a popular proverb that the children were suffering for the sins of their fathers. The message here is clear: Don't blame others for the mistakes you make. God doesn't will the suffering our actions produce, but we still have to deal with it.

Teenagers, like many adults, are quick to blame others for their problems. Accepting responsibility for their actions is difficult. Teenagers need to understand that they do have freedom in Christ—but they also must live within limits so they don't have to live with negative consequences.

THIS LESSON AT A GLANCE

Section	Minutes	What Students Will Do	Supplies
Opener (Option 1)	5 to 10	**The Sex Test**—Take a test to see how much they know about the dangers of sex.	"The Sex Test" handout (p. 42), pencils
(Option 2)		**Real-Life Story**—Talk with someone who's had to deal with the negative consequences of sexual activity.	
Action and Reflection	10 to 15	**Risky Business**—Play a game to experience the consequences of risky sexual behavior.	Copies of "Consequences" box (p. 38), scissors, box, egg timer (or other countdown timer)
Bible Application	10 to 15	**Consequences**—Discover what the Bible has to say about responsibility and consequences.	Copies of "Scripture Questions" box (p. 39), Bibles
Commitment	10 to 15	**Case Studies**—Discuss case studies of teenagers who made poor sexual decisions.	Pencils, paper
Closing (Option 1)	up to 5	**Body Affirmations**—Draw outlines of themselves and write affirmations in them.	Markers, large sheets of newsprint, tape
(Option 2)		**Pushing Back the Danger**—Experience overcoming a temptation and receive encouragement from each other.	Candy bar

The Lesson

Before the Lesson

If you want to use Option 2 as the opener, arrange ahead of time to have a teenage mother or father attend the class. Brief her or him ahead of time about the nature of the class. See Option 2 for more details.

☐ OPTION 1: THE SEX TEST

Distribute "The Sex Test" handout (p. 42) and pencils to your class. Say: **All of us want to believe we know all there is to know about sex. But how much do we know about the dangers that go with sex? Let's find out.**

Have teenagers complete the test. Then go over the questions one by one. Use the following procedure:

1. Read the statement aloud and have the class members say whether the statement is true or false. See how many voted each way.

2. Give the correct answer from the "Answer Box," then let the group members briefly share their reactions to the answer.

After discussing each question, say: **The pleasure of sex is a well-discussed topic among teenagers and adults alike. But people often ignore the dangers of sex. Today we'll look at how we can make responsible decisions to avoid the dangers of sex.**

☐ OPTION 2: REAL-LIFE STORY

Arrange for someone who's had to deal with the consequences of sexual activity to speak to the class—preferably a teenage mother or father. A local high school counselor would be a good resource. Ask the speaker to tell her or his story, but not to be too melodramatic or use scare tactics. When kids arrive, have the speaker briefly tell her or his story. Then allow kids to ask a few questions before diving into the rest of the lesson.

Say: **As you just heard, the fun of sex can also include difficult and negative consequences. Today we're going to discuss how we can avoid those consequences.**

O P E N E R
(5 to 10 minutes)

Answer Box

1. True.
2. True.
3. True, as of 1990.
4. False, it's not 100 percent effective.
5. False.
6. True.
7. False. Although condoms reduce the chance for getting a disease, there is still a possibility of getting one.
8. True.
9. True.
10. True.
11. False. At least 10 STDs have been identified.
12. False.
13. True.
14. True.
15. False. If you're careful, you can greatly reduce the chances. But abstinence is the only foolproof method.

ACTION AND REFLECTION
(10 to 15 minutes)

RISKY BUSINESS

Copy the "Consequences" box, and cut it apart. Fold the slips and place them in a box. Form a circle and ask:

● **What are risks people take when they "play around" sexually?**

Have the class mention several, then say: **Today we're going to play a game called Risky Business. An egg timer will be set and then placed inside a box. We'll pass the box around the circle, never knowing when the timer will go off. In the game, we're going to assume that all of us have become sexually active. We are all "doing it." As long as the box is going around and the timer hasn't gone off, we're all "playing around" sexually with no problems. But when the timer goes off, whoever has the box has to face the consequences of sexual freedom.**

Set the countdown timer for 10 to 30 seconds, and place it in the box along with the "Consequences" slips. Any timer that can be set to go off will work. Some watches might work too. Begin passing the box around the circle. Whoever has the box when it goes off must then draw a slip of paper from the box, read it aloud and say what he or she would do if really in that situation.

Play several rounds. Each time, set the timer for a different amount of time—from 10 to 30 seconds. If you don't have time for all the slips to be drawn, stop the game and read the rest of the consequences aloud.

Ask:

● **How did you feel as the box was passed around?** (Nervous; uncomfortable; anxious.)

● **How is that like the feeling people have when they take chances sexually? Explain.** (It's very similar—you don't know what you're getting into; it's not the same at all—there's less chance involved.)

● **How did you feel if you had to choose a consequence?** (Angry; it was unfair; upset; it didn't bother me.)

● **How did you feel if you never had to suffer one of the consequences?** (Relieved; lucky; happy.)

● **Which consequences of sexual activity scare you the most?** Explain.

Say: **Consequences aren't new to our day and age. In Bible times, people often dealt with negative consequences of their behavior.**

Consequences

Copy this box. Then cut apart each item for the Risky Business game.

1. Nothing happens—there are no consequences—yet. How do you feel?

2. Your parents found condoms or birth control pills in your room. They confront you. What do you say?

3. You are (or your girlfriend is) pregnant. What do you say to your parents? your friends?

4. The person you had sex with lost interest in you as soon as you slept with him or her. How do you feel?

5. You have (or your partner has) been using a condom for birth control. The company that manufactures your brand has just issued a recall because the product is defective. What do you do?

6. You have the sexually transmitted disease chlamydia. One of the possibilities is that you'll become sterile. What do you say to your partner? your parents?

7. The person you had sex with is now telling everyone in your school about what happened. How do you respond?

8. The person you had sex with has just been diagnosed with AIDS. How do you feel?

CONSEQUENCES

Form groups of no more than six. Copy the "Scripture Questions" box, and give each group one of the two sections: Genesis 2:15-17 or Ezekiel 18:26-32. Have groups each read their scripture and answer the questions in the box.

Form two groups—one with all the groups that worked on the Genesis passage and one with all the groups that worked on the Ezekiel passage. Have groups each come up with a brief skit (no more than 30 seconds) to demonstrate the meaning of their passage.

After the groups perform their skits, ask:

● **What are the limits God sets for our sexual behavior?** (Don't have sex before marriage; don't do anything that could be dangerous.)

● **Why do you think God placed these limits on us?** (They're for our own good; God doesn't want us to have any fun.)

● **Why are some consequences irreversible?** (Because they're always in our memories; because you have to live with your mistakes.)

Say: **We live with the consequences of our decisions. But what if we've already made mistakes? How should we respond? Next we'll take a look at a couple of situations where teenagers did mess up. And we'll determine the course of action they should take.**

CASE STUDIES

Read each of the following case studies aloud. For each, ask:

● **What could this person have done to avoid this problem?**

● **What should this person do now?**

● **What would God's response be to this situation?**

CASE STUDIES

Jim and Terri

Jim and Terri are both seniors and have been dating for over a year. They hope to get married someday, but they want to go to college and get degrees first. As they've dated, their relationship has gradually become more and more intimate. Last night, "it just happened." They hadn't planned on having sex. They didn't take any precautions. Terri is concerned that she might be pregnant.

Laura and Shane

Shane met Laura at a party. She was beautiful, said all the right things and before the night was over he'd

---

Scripture Questions

Read aloud Genesis 2:15-17. Then discuss these questions in your group:

● Why does God put limits on our freedom?

● What are the limits to our freedom?

● What happens when we go beyond those limits?

- - - - - - - - - - - - - - - - - - - -

Read aloud Ezekiel 18:26-32. Then discuss these questions in your group:

● Who's responsible and accountable for human behavior?

● When we live outside the boundaries, what happens?

● Why does God allow the consequences of our actions to fall on us?

COMMITMENT
(10 to 15 minutes)

slept with her. It was his first time. Later, he found out Laura had slept with a lot of guys.

In his health class, Shane's teacher made the comment that if you have sex with someone, you've slept with everyone they've slept with. Shane's terrified. He could've been exposed to any of several diseases, including AIDS.

Marie

Marie never felt loved or accepted by her family. All her life she's been looking for affection and attention. In junior high she learned she could get attention from boys by giving them what they wanted physically. Marie can't even count the number of people she's had sex with. Lately Marie has realized what she found with guys wasn't love. She's still lonely. She still feels unloved. Actually, she feels even worse than before. She's lost respect for herself.

After brief discussion of all the situations, ask:
● **What can each of us do to protect ourselves from the consequences of sexual activity?** (Abstain from sex; avoid situations where sexual temptation is high.)

Say: **There really is no such thing as "safe sex." All sexual behavior involves risk.**

Hand out pencils and paper, and have kids each write a covenant with God expressing their commitment to choose responsible sexual behavior. Let kids know they won't have to tell what they write.

Say: **No matter what your sexual history is, you can begin a new commitment to God to maintain responsible sexuality. He loves you just as you are and can help you stick to your commitment.**

☐ OPTION 1: BODY AFFIRMATIONS

Hand each class member a marker and a sheet of newsprint longer than the person is tall. Have teenagers each find a partner and take turns lying on the newsprint as their partner outlines their body. Have kids each put their name on their newsprint. Then tape the newsprint outlines to the wall.

Allow kids several minutes to write positive things about each other on the body outlines. Have them each think of some positive quality or characteristic the person expressed during the last four weeks.

Have the group form a circle, and have class members each read one comment from their outline that means the most to them. Close with prayer.

CLOSING
(up to 5 minutes)

☐ OPTION 2: PUSHING BACK THE DANGER

Form a circle. Give a candy bar to someone in the circle. Tell him or her not to eat it. Say: **Just as it may be tempting to eat this candy bar, sex is tempting. But with God's help—and each other's help—we can push back the danger and avoid making poor sex decisions.**

Have group members call out to the person holding the candy bar positive words of encouragement to make good sex decisions. For example, kids may say, "You can avoid sexual pressures" or "I know you can wait until marriage." Then have that person pass the candy bar to the person on his or her right. Continue the process of passing the candy bar and calling out encouragement until the candy bar comes back to where it began.

Place the candy bar in the center of the circle and close with prayer, asking God to help each person make responsible sex decisions. Place the candy bar in a prominent place in your meeting room to remind kids to "just say wait" to sex.

If You Still Have Time . . .

Mistake Talk—Form groups of no more than five. Have kids talk about how they feel when they hear of someone who has AIDS (or another sexually transmitted disease) or is pregnant.

Course Reflection—Form a circle. Ask students to reflect on the past four lessons. Have them take turns completing the following sentences:

- Something I learned in this course was . . .
- If I could tell my friends about this course, I'd say . . .
- Something I'll do differently because of this course is . . .

THE **Sex** TEST

Each of the following statements involves the risks that go with sexual behavior. Circle your answers and see how many you know.

	True	False
1. Gonorrhea is a treatable sexually transmitted disease, but it may result in sterility or kidney damage.	True	False
2. You can die from syphilis.	True	False
3. There is no cure for AIDS.	True	False
4. If you use a condom you can't get pregnant.	True	False
5. Spermicidal chemicals—such as foams—are safer than condoms.	True	False
6. Chlamydia is a sexually transmitted disease.	True	False
7. If you use a condom you're safe from sexually transmitted diseases.	True	False
8. The only people who are totally safe from sexually transmitted diseases are two virgins who marry, remain faithful and avoid injected drugs.	True	False
9. You can get the AIDS virus from a heterosexual relationship.	True	False
10. The rhythm method—not having sex during the time when the woman is fertile—is the least effective form of birth control.	True	False
11. There are only four kinds of sexually transmitted diseases.	True	False
12. If you wash carefully after intercourse you can't get a sexually transmitted disease or get pregnant.	True	False
13. The most common sexually transmitted disease is gonorrhea.	True	False
14. Genital herpes, a sexually transmitted disease that resembles cold sores, is treatable but incurable.	True	False
15. If you're careful, you can be sexually active and still avoid sexually transmitted diseases.	True	False

BONUS IDEAS

Doc Talk—Have a physician talk to the class about the physical aspects of sex and sexuality. Have teenagers turn in written questions they have about their bodies, the physical aspects of sex and sexuality, birth control and sexually transmitted diseases.

Teenage Parent Talk—Invite a teenage parent to talk to the class about the realities that go with parenting a child.

Right or Wrong Game—Have teenagers write on 3×5 cards sexual behaviors they're uncertain about such as: French kissing; fondling genitals; sensuous dancing. Collect the cards. Then shuffle and turn them upside down.

Have each class member draw a card and read it. Then have that teenager choose one of the following statements as the appropriate response to the behavior:
1. This behavior is okay for teenagers.
2. This behavior is only okay for married couples.
3. This behavior isn't okay for anyone.

The class can then try to argue with or support the teenager's choice. Be sure all teenagers have a turn to participate.

If you and the class are uncertain about some of the behaviors' acceptability, consult your pastor. Bring the answers and the church's position to the next class. Use scripture to support your views. Read and discuss how the following scriptures apply to the issues: Matthew 5:27-28; Romans 13:13-14; and 1 Corinthians 7:2-5.

Current Movie—Have the class go to a current movie that deals with sexual issues. Afterward, discuss the sexual issues in the movie. Consult with parents to let them know in advance the movie you plan to take kids to see. If appropriate, invite parents to attend and help in the discussion too. Be informed of the movie's rating before seeing it. Make sure that's acceptable to parents.

Marriage Inventory—Obtain a premarital inventory or counseling checklist pastors and counselors use to help couples identify issues and values in their relationship. Have the class take the inventory to see what kind of issues are important in marriage.

Centipede Partners—Have class members sit facing each other in two parallel lines of chairs. Toss out a topic that relates to sex, such as "what I like in a member of the opposite

MEETINGS AND MORE

sex." Allow 30 seconds to a minute for each partner to talk about the topic. On "rotate," have everyone move one chair clockwise and sit down with a new partner and a new topic.

Shadow Thoughts—Do a role play in which two characters have a discussion on a sexual topic; for example, someone asking another person for a date, or two members of the same sex talking about how good-looking a member of the opposite sex is. Choose two "shadows"—one for each character. Have the shadows each stand behind their character. Each time one of the characters in the skit speaks, the shadow says what he or she believes the character is really thinking. This can be hilarious—and insightful.

Confidential Sex Surveys—Give class members copies of the "Sex and Faith" handout (p. 46) and a supply of stamped envelopes with the church's address on them. Have kids give the surveys to friends, parents, church members and other people to complete and return. Remind kids to tell the survey participants the surveys are to be done anonymously. After getting the surveys back, compile and discuss the results.

Dear Counselor—Have teenagers anonymously write letters to "Dear Counselor" that deal with real issues they're facing. Read the letters aloud to the class, and have the class members respond to the letters as counselors. Or invite a Christian counselor to respond to the letters.

Situation Skits—Have class members write on 3×5 cards situations they face that involve sexual issues. Choose several situations, and have groups create skits based on the cards. Follow each skit with a discussion.

Peer Interviews—Have class members informally interview kids in their school about a sexual issue such as premarital sex, birth control or sexually transmitted diseases. The following Sunday have the class report and discuss its findings.

Table Talk—Use the "Table Talk" handout (p. 19) as a basis for a parents and teenagers' meeting following the last session. Distribute the handout before the meeting. Open the lesson with a couple of fun, low-risk crowdbreakers. For crowdbreaker ideas, check out *Quick Crowdbreakers and Games for Youth Groups* (Group Books). Begin the discussion by having each teenager paired with someone else's parent. Then move to sharing between parents and teenagers in the same family.

Dating Contracts—Have class members each create dating contracts in which they say what they expect of a member of the opposite sex on a date and what they're willing to give. Make sure this is done in the context of a discussion on respecting the other person's feelings and values.

Parents and Kids' Retreat—Have a retreat for teenagers and their parents. Include times when daughters can talk with their mothers, sons can talk with their fathers, daughters can talk with their fathers, and sons can talk with their mothers about sexual issues. Be sure to have qualified volunteers help facilitate the discussions in the various groups.

Include fun games at the beginning of the retreat so kids and parents can get comfortable with each other. Be sure to focus on the positive aspects of sexuality as well as the negative. Use this retreat to help parents and kids better understand an appropriate faith response to their sexuality.

RETREAT IDEA

✦SEX✦AND✦FAITH✦

Our senior high class at church has been studying sexuality and how it relates to our faith. We want to know what you think. Please complete the following brief survey and return it to us in the envelope provided. Please *don't* include your name or address with the survey. Thanks for your cooperation.

How do you react when someone mentions sex or you read about sex in a book or magazine?
☐ I'm interested.   ☐ I'm embarrassed.
☐ I'm intrigued.   ☐ It doesn't affect me.
☐ I'm shocked.

Which statement best describes what *your church* teaches about sex?
☐ Sex outside of marriage is always wrong.   ☐ Sex outside of marriage is usually wrong.
☐ Sex is okay if two people love each other.

Which of the following statements best describes how *you* feel about sex?
☐ Sex outside of marriage is always wrong.   ☐ Sex outside of marriage is usually wrong.
☐ Sex is okay if two people love each other.

Mark your degree of agreement with the following statements by checking the appropriate box.

	Agree	Not sure	Disagree
1. Movies and television portray an accurate view of sex.	☐	☐	☐
2. Sex should not be enjoyed, it's only for reproduction.	☐	☐	☐
3. My parents taught me all I need to know about sex.	☐	☐	☐
4. Making out is okay for two unmarried people in love.	☐	☐	☐
5. Sexuality is more than sexual intercourse.	☐	☐	☐
6. The church in general teaches that sex is bad.	☐	☐	☐
7. I've had sexual thoughts I've been ashamed of.	☐	☐	☐
8. Masturbation is a sin.	☐	☐	☐
9. My faith is important in shaping my view of sex.	☐	☐	☐
10. God wants people to remain virgins until they're married.	☐	☐	☐

The following questions are very personal. Please answer honestly—remember your survey will be anonymous.

● If you've never been married:

Have you ever had sexual intercourse?
☐ Yes   ☐ No

If you have, how do you feel about it now?
☐ I'm ashamed.   ☐ I'm proud.   ☐ I'm confused.   ☐ I'm disgusted.   ☐ It doesn't bother me.

● If you've been married:

Did you have sexual intercourse before marriage?
☐ Yes   ☐ No

If yes, how do you feel about it now?
☐ I'm ashamed.   ☐ I'm proud.   ☐ I'm confused.   ☐ I'm disgusted.   ☐ It doesn't bother me.

Do you believe your attitude toward sex and sexuality affects your relationship with God?
☐ Yes   ☐ No

CURRICULUM REORDER—TOP PRIORITY

Order now to prepare for your upcoming Sunday school classes, youth ministry meetings and weekend retreats! Each book includes all teacher and student materials—plus photocopiable handouts—for any size class.

FOR SENIOR HIGH:

Quantity

_____ **Christians in a Non-Christian World**
ISBN 1-55945-224-2

_____ **Counterfeit Religions**
ISBN 1-55945-207-2

_____ **Dating Decisions**
ISBN 1-55945-215-3

_____ **Exodus: Following God**
ISBN 1-55945-226-9

_____ **Exploring Ethical Issues**
ISBN 1-55945-225-0

_____ **Faith for Tough Times**
ISBN 1-55945-216-1

_____ **Forgiveness**
ISBN 1-55945-223-4

_____ **Getting Along With Parents**
ISBN 1-55945-202-1

_____ **The Gospel of John: Jesus' Teachings**
ISBN 1-55945-208-0

_____ **Hazardous to Your Health: AIDS, Steroids & Eating Disorders**
ISBN 1-55945-200-5

_____ **Is Marriage in Your Future?**
ISBN 1-55945-203-X

_____ **Jesus' Death & Resurrection**
ISBN 1-55945-211-0

_____ **The Joy of Serving**
ISBN 1-55945-210-2

Quantity

_____ **Knowing God's Will**
ISBN 1-55945-205-6

_____ **Life After High School**
ISBN 1-55945-220-X

_____ **Making Good Decisions**
ISBN 1-55945-209-9

_____ **Money: A Christian Perspective**
ISBN 1-55945-212-9

_____ **Movies, Music, TV & Me**
ISBN 1-55945-213-7

_____ **Overcoming Insecurities**
ISBN 1-55945-221-8

_____ **Responding to Injustice**
ISBN 1-55945-214-5

_____ **School Struggles**
ISBN 1-55945-201-3

_____ **Sex: A Christian Perspective**
ISBN 1-55945-206-4

_____ **What Is the Church?**
ISBN 1-55945-222-6

_____ **Who Is God?**
ISBN 1-55945-218-8

_____ **Who Is Jesus?**
ISBN 1-55945-219-6

_____ **Who Is the Holy Spirit?**
ISBN 1-55945-217-X

_____ **Your Life as a Disciple**
ISBN 1-55945-204-8

FOR JUNIOR HIGH/MIDDLE SCHOOL:

Quantity

_____ **Accepting Others: Beyond Barriers & Stereotypes**
ISBN 1-55945-126-2

_____ **Applying the Bible to Life**
ISBN 1-55945-116-5

_____ **Becoming Responsible**
ISBN 1-55945-109-2

_____ **Boosting Self-Esteem**
ISBN 1-55945-100-9

_____ **Caring for God's Creation**
ISBN 1-55945-121-1

_____ **Christmas: A Fresh Look**
ISBN 1-55945-124-6

_____ **Dealing With Death**
ISBN 1-55945-112-2

_____ **Drugs & Drinking**
ISBN 1-55945-118-1

_____ **Evil and the Occult**
ISBN 1-55945-102-5

_____ **Genesis: The Beginnings**
ISBN 1-55945-111-4

_____ **Guys & Girls: Understanding Each Other**
ISBN 1-55945-110-6

_____ **Handling Conflict**
ISBN 1-55945-125-4

_____ **Heaven & Hell**
ISBN 1-55945-131-9

Quantity

_____ **Is God Unfair?**
ISBN 1-55945-108-4

_____ **Love or Infatuation?**
ISBN 1-55945-128-9

_____ **Making Parents Proud**
ISBN 1-55945-107-6

_____ **Making the Most of School**
ISBN 1-55945-113-0

_____ **Materialism**
ISBN 1-55945-130-0

_____ **Miracles!**
ISBN 1-55945-117-3

_____ **Peace & War**
ISBN 1-55945-123-8

_____ **Peer Pressure**
ISBN 1-55945-103-3

_____ **Prayer**
ISBN 1-55945-104-1

_____ **Sermon on the Mount**
ISBN 1-55945-129-7

_____ **Telling Your Friends About Christ**
ISBN 1-55945-114-9

_____ **The Ten Commandments**
ISBN 1-55945-127-0

_____ **Today's Music: Good or Bad?**
ISBN 1-55945-101-7

_____ **What's a Christian?**
ISBN 1-55945-105-X

Order today from your favorite bookstore, or write: Group Publishing, Box 485, Loveland, CO 80539. For mail orders, please add postage/handling of $3 for orders up to $15, $4 for orders of $15.01+. Colorado residents add 3% sales tax.

NOW YOU CAN TEACH ACTIVE BIBLE LESSONS TO 5TH- AND 6TH-GRADERS...

...with Group's NEW **Hands-On Bible Curriculum™**

Make learning fun and watch your kids' enthusiasm for the Bible grow!

Group's new **Hands-On Bible Curriculum™** will help you teach the Bible in a whole new way. Your 5th- and 6th-graders will pay attention to your lesson. They'll be more eager to learn. You'll teach lessons your kids understand and really apply to their daily lives—because Group's **Hands-On Bible Curriculum™** uses lively active learning experiences, not passive lecture, to bring home the Bible truth.

In each session, your students will participate in a variety of fun and memorable learning experiences using discovery tools you've not seen with any other curriculum. These fascinating gadgets and gizmos help your 5th- and 6th-graders discover biblical truths and <u>remember</u> what they learn—because they're <u>doing</u> instead of just listening.

Save yourself time and money with these complete discovery-packed kits!

While your students are learning more, you'll be working less—simply following the quick and easy instructions in the Teachers Guide. Lesson-planning is a cinch with Group's **Hands-On Bible Curriculum™** You'll get plenty of material for a fast-paced 35- to 60-minute session. And, if you still have time, there's an arsenal of Bonus Ideas and Time Stuffers to keep kids occupied—and learning!

In addition to the easy-to-use Teachers Guide, you'll get all the essential teaching materials you need in a ready-to-use kit called the **Learning Lab™**. No more running from store to store hunting for lesson materials—all the active-learning tools you need are included in the **Learning Lab™**. You'll get everything you need to teach 13 exciting Bible lessons to any size class! Plus, you'll SAVE BIG over other curriculum programs that require you to buy expensive separate student books—all student handouts may be photocopied from the included masters.

Capture your kids' attention with 3 interesting topics every 13 weeks!

Group's **Hands-On Bible Curriculum™** covers topics that support the needs of your young people—as well as your church's need to teach the Bible with integrity. Every quarter you'll explore 3 meaningful subjects. One is centered around learning about <u>others</u>... another helps your students learn about <u>themselves</u>... and a third teaches your kids about <u>God</u>. Switching topics every month keeps your 5th- and 6th-graders enthused and coming back for more. The full 2-year program will help your kids...

- make God-pleasing lifestyle choices
- appreciate their God-given potential
- seek to grow as Christians
- ask for God's help in daily decisions

Take the boredom out of Sunday school, children's church, mid-week meetings and youth group for your 5th- and 6th-graders... and make your teachers' jobs easier and more rewarding... with no-fail lessons that are ready in a flash! Order Group's **Hands-On Bible Curriculum™** for your 5th- and 6th-graders today.

Group's **Hands-On Bible Curriculum™**, Quarter 1

Friendships
Self-Esteem
God's Love

Teachers Guide	ISBN 1-55945-300-1	$14.95
Learning Lab™	ISBN 1-55945-301-X	$34.95

Order today from your favorite bookstore, or write: Group Publishing, Box 485, Loveland, CO 80539. For mail orders, please add postage/handling of $3 for orders up to $15, $4 for orders of $15.01+. Colorado residents add 3% sales tax.